Craniosacral Therapy 101

Understand Biodynamic Rhythm, Tissue Intelligence, & Harmonizing of Energetic Body with Touchstone Techniques to Attain Holistic Self-Healing & Trauma Resolution

Jonathan Shaper

Table of Contents

Introduction 1

Discovering Craniosacral Therapy.......................... 5

    The history and principles of craniosacral therapy
.... 5

Craniosacral System Self-Healing......................... 7

The Mind-Body Connection..................................... 9

    Negative Mind-Body Outcomes 10

The Craniosacral System...13

    Cerebrospinal Fluid and Dura Mater....................15

    Self-Regulation of the Craniosacral System..........16

Biodynamic Craniosacral Therapy.........................17

    Biodynamic Rhythm.. 18

    The Principles of Biodynamic Therapy.................19

The Breath of Life..21

    Breath of Life Exercises...................................... 22

Harmonizing the Energetic Body........................... 25

    Energy Balancing... 27

Craniosacral Therapy Techniques 29

The Light Touch 29

Listening to the Craniosacral Rhythm.................32

Cranial Bone Manipulation................................33

Fascial Unwinding 35

    The unwinding process 36

Sacral Rocking...37

    The sacral rocking technique 38

Breathwork..38

    Diaphragmatic breathing 38

    Somatic experiencing breathwork 39

    Balanced breathing....................................39

    Four-part breath.......................................40

    Ujjayi breath technique 41

Visualization..41

Resolving Trauma..45

    Somatic Awareness Exercise...........................47

    Gentle Neck Release Exercise 48

    Stillness and Self-Folding Exercise....................49

Boosting Tissue Intelligence................................51

Conclusion 53

References...55

Introduction

I had experienced chronic migraines for years and tried everything. Still, the pain loomed over me, spontaneously manifesting itself and taking over huge chunks of my days. That was until I stumbled perchance, onto craniosacral therapy.

Ever the skeptic, I went into a session with a practitioner I'd found in my area through an online search. But as I lay there at the beginning of the session, and as the therapist gently placed her hands on my temple, I felt myself relax into her soothing touch.

In that session, I felt a profound sense of release, like the pain that had taken over my life was slowly but surely unwinding.

From then on, the migraines became less frequent, and the pangs less intense. In the years since, I can go for weeks, even months before I get a fairly dull migraine, which predictably dissipates once I perform my favorite self-care craniosacral therapy techniques.

I've become an ardent practitioner of craniosacral therapy, both in session with holistic healers and by myself, or sometimes with a partner.

Once you understand the fundamentals of how this holistic healing technique works, and learn how to carry out a few techniques on your own, you will never look back.

And it's not just for sufferers of migraines either. Craniosacral therapy reduces stress and it's known to promote deep relaxation and relieve anxiety. This is why it's often sought out by trauma survivors and people battling through heightened emotional states.

It's known to elicit release of emotional and physical trauma that's stored in the body, along with negative energy, helping people process and heal from the past experiences that haunt them and limit their lives.

When it comes to pain, beyond migraines, CST (craniosacral therapy) also helps heal and manage chronic and tension headaches, and other forms of pain in the head and neck area.

CST makes you more aware of your body, and it helps you pinpoint and resolve blockages that result from both physical and emotional issues.

CST supports the regulation of the autonomic nervous system, which is dysregulated in many people, particularly those who've lived through intensive traumatic experiences.

CST also improves the quality of your sleep and helps with insomnia. Sleep, as you know, is critical for your overall well-being and recovery from both physical and emotional trauma.

CST makes you a lot more emotionally resilient, as it restores both physical and emotional balance in the body. It can be a healthy emotional coping mechanism on its own and can complement other mechanisms.

CST turns people on to self-care. Learning craniosacral therapy equips you with self-healing techniques, and empowers you to take an increasingly active approach to your own well-being.

Craniosacral therapy is a holistic form of healing, meaning it takes into account the interconnectedness of the mind and the body. It's also completely non-invasive, and very gentle.

As I started trying out holistic practices, I worried about how invasive some of them appeared to be, and was drawn to CST because it didn't require needles to be stuck in my body as was the case with acupuncture, or complex physical exercises like kundalini yoga. All it takes are gentle but technically precise touches to the head and spinal area. It asks very little of you to try it out, and there's really no potential downside.

More than anything though, craniosacral therapy is empowering. Imagine being able to soothe yourself and relieve tension whenever it arises. Imagine being able to work on your own physical and emotional trauma, and reduce it with each passing day until you attain inner tranquility. That is the promise of craniosacral therapy.

Your self-healing journey may take a lot of holistic practices, but allow me to persuade you in this book that craniosacral therapy ought to be an integral part of that journey. It works best when it's integrated with other therapeutic approaches, and it's done by trained practitioners, but there are plenty of things you can learn on your own with this book as a resource, and practice them without fear of accidental harm, but with a great chance for relief and self-healing.

As we go on, we will systematically discuss all the concepts that you need to know to be fully introduced to the practice of craniosacral therapy. We will also teach you exercises that you can use on your own to unlock your body's self-healing powers, as well as those that can only be done with technical assistance from a licensed craniosacral therapist.

By the end of this book, you will have functional knowledge of the practice of craniosacral therapy, and you can then build from there, either as a client or as someone looking to go into craniosacral therapy as a career path.

Thank you for choosing this book, and let's get started.

Discovering Craniosacral Therapy

Even the most renowned craniosacral therapists will admit that there isn't much complexity to the practice. It is defined as a gentle, hands-on holistic approach that activates and promotes the body's very own healing abilities. It's based on the understanding that your mind, body, and spirit are interconnected and that restoring balance and harmony in the craniosacral system allows healing in all these areas.

The history and principles of craniosacral therapy

In the early 20th century, Dr. William Sutherland proposed the theory that the bones that make up the skull can be moved, ever so subtly, and that the movement and position of these bones are related to the overall health of the person's entire body[i].

Craniosacral therapy is rooted in a genre of alternative medicine known as osteopathy which focuses on the underrated importance of the musculoskeletal system in keeping us healthy.

It was Dr. John E. Upledger, an osteopathic doctor, who came up with the established principle of craniosacral therapy in the 1970s. Most of his practice, research, and education are carried out by the Upledger Institute which he founded to promote the therapy[ii].

The core principles of craniosacral therapy can be summarized in the following concepts:

The craniosacral rhythm - Practitioners of craniosacral therapy believe that the cerebrospinal fluid around the human brain and the spinal cord has a subtle rhythmic movement. CST involves detecting, perceiving, and working with this rhythm to heal and promote well-being.

The body's self-healing ability - CST is based on the understanding that the body can naturally heal itself, and the gentle touches applied merely facilitate this self-healing process by removing blockages in the craniosacral system.

The holistic approach principle - CST uses the holistic approach meaning that the emotional and spiritual elements of the person being healed are considered alongside the physical elements. The goal is to harmonize and balance the 'whole" person, as well-being cannot be attained by only focusing on the physical.

The gentle touch principle - As mentioned, CST is done using very gentle non-invasive touch, both in evaluating the person and in treating them. Very light pressure is applied to the cranial bones, a practice known as 'listening.' The idea is not to manipulate the body but to pay attention to the signs it's sending.

The principle of individualized treatment - CST sessions are tailored to the specific person being healed. The therapist may focus on a specific area, but it's never the same for two patients. The craniosacral therapy approach may recognize general principles, but the practice itself is personalized to one's needs.

The complementary approach - Craniosacral therapy is meant to complement rather than replace other forms of therapy or conventional medical treatment. It supports healing, but one must always seek the help of medical professionals instead of fully relying on this or other holistic approaches.

Continual learning principle - Expertise in CST requires continual learning, training, research, and discovery. This is a relatively novel but drastically evolving area in holistic healing, and it is good to always read new books, follow seasoned practitioners, and learn through practice.

Regulatory bodies and medical establishments treat all forms of holistic healing (including craniosacral therapy) with a lot of skepticism, so practicing or trying it out requires one to open oneself to new possibilities and to do so of their own accord. But there's growing scientific literature that explains these principles in depth. In fact, studies have continuously shown that holistic practices do in fact promote healing[iii].

Craniosacral System Self-Healing

The craniosacral system refers to the parts of the human physiological makeup, including the cerebrospinal fluid, the membranes that engulf both the brain and the spinal cord, and the bones that make up the skull, and spine, all the way to the sacrum. The sacrum is a triangle-shaped bone located at the base of the spine (also known as the tailbone).

The cerebrospinal fluid is produced by ventricles that pass through the brain and the spinal cord. It provides a protective cushion around these sensitive organs and gives the brain buoyancy. It's also responsible for supplying nutrients to the brain and spinal cord.

As mentioned, the cerebrospinal fluid is responsible for the craniosacral rhythm. This occurs as the fluid is produced and absorbed, and moves back and forth, bathing and protecting the brain and spine.

Given the vital nature of the organ systems serviced by the craniosacral system, having it in a good state of balance has numerous positive impacts on one's health and well-being.

The system has an innate self-regulatory and self-healing mechanism, where it maintains its own balance, fixing any disharmony that may occur. These natural self-healing abilities can be hindered by tension, blockages, and other restrictions, hence the need for craniosacral therapy.

The craniosacral system is irrevocably tied to the nervous system function because the organs it protects and balances are the components of the central nervous system. The nervous system itself reaches all across the body. That's why craniosacral therapy can have positive wellness outcomes in areas of the body further away from the head and spine.

While the efficacy of the underlying mechanism of the craniosacral therapeutic practice is yet to be conclusively demonstrated through empirical findings, many people report a wide array of positive outcomes from the practice[iv].

The Mind-Body Connection

Your mind and body are interconnected in intricate ways. Emotions have a bearing on your physical health. If you are stressed, traumatized, or experiencing other negative emotions, these conditions can physically manifest themselves in the form of pain, tension in the muscles, or problems with digestion. It's therefore demonstrably true that one's state of mind impacts the body in a very direct way.

This connection between the mind and body is a pathway for the body to heal itself when you address the mental stressors. To that end, craniosacral therapy sessions pursue emotional release, where the aim is to find deeply buried emotions and memories and to let go of them.

CST is based on the understanding that emotional trauma is stored in the body (tissues, muscles, and the craniosacral system itself), and so unresolved trauma leads to discomfort or more serious physical symptoms.

CST practitioners are always keen to avoid re-traumatization of their patients, and they generally practice trauma-informed care. They always create an ambiance to make you feel safe and supported, which facilitates emotional release as opposed to compounding the trauma.

To heal, the mind and body must be integrated. Harmony between different aspects of one's being is restored when the imbalance in the disordered component is addressed. This means you can heal the emotional by healing the physical, and vice versa.

Negative Mind-Body Outcomes

Your emotional and physical health are interlinked in complex and dynamic ways. One influences the other, and vice versa.

Scientists have established that emotional states such as chronic stress, anxiety, and depression can ignite stress responses in the body. If these responses are activated for a long time, there's overproduction of the stress hormone cortisol, which floods your system and has negative effects on various parts of the body. Common outcomes of this reaction include a weak immune system, high blood pressure, and gastrointestinal (digestion) problems.

It's also a well-known fact that prolonged periods of emotional distress or negative emotion can lead to chronic inflammation, which is associated with diabetes, cardiovascular diseases, and autoimmune disorders. Stress is known to increase the amount of inflammatory markers, compounding underlying health problems.

It's also been discovered that chronic stress suppresses the immune response, making people more vulnerable to illness and infection. One's emotional state has a bearing on their ability to get physically ill.

Emotional state also influences how we perceive pain. Negative emotions (stress, depression) make pain feel worse, while positive emotional states (relaxation, etc.) can have analgesic effects.

Emotions also have physical outcomes in terms of the quality of sleep we get, the types of coping mechanisms we choose in life (emotions could lead to drug abuse which is a physical outcome), and our habits in general. In the inverse, physical health also impacts emotional well-being. Having a physical disability, or experiencing physical pain, can lead to emotional distress, depression, anxiety, and a worse quality of life.

When we take medication for purposes of improving our physical health, they often have side effects that negatively impact our emotions or mood.

Our physical appearance or the state of our bodies has an impact on our body image and self-esteem. Here, there's a direct link between the physical body and the emotional (what's in the mind).

The mind-body connection is a vivid reality for all of us, which is why some spiritual traditions make no distinction between the two. The holistic approach is based on the understanding that they all must be considered at the same time, and in consideration of the other. Besides craniosacral therapy, practices such as yoga, psychotherapy, meditation, mindfulness, and even the teachings of most religions, consider the mind and body as irrevocably intertwined. They seek to bridge the gap between mind and body to make us well-rounded persons.

The Craniosacral System

Now, let's take a deeper dive into the craniosacral system to understand it better.

The craniosacral system has a lot more components than the general ones we've mentioned, and each one factors into craniosacral therapy in its own unique way. The cerebrospinal fluid is the clear and colorless liquid that we said provides nutrients to the brain, protects it, and keeps it buoyant.

The dura mater is a tough fibrous membrane that encloses the brain and spinal cord, and it serves as the container for the cerebral spinal fluid.

There's also the arachnoid membrane, which is a thin, web-like layer located beneath the dura mater. It helps encase the brain and spinal cord and contributes to the movement of the cerebrospinal fluid.

The membrane layers covering the brain and spinal cord are collectively known as the meninges. The innermost of these layers is the pia mater. It adheres to the surface of the other membranes and it's the one in direct contact with the spinal fluid.

In fact, the craniosacral system has a network of membranes and connective tissue, including the falx cerebri, and the tentorium cerebelli, all of which influence how the cerebrospinal fluid moves about.

The bones that make up the skull are known as cranial bones, and they too, including the cranial vault, are components of the craniosacral system. In craniosacral therapy literature, these bones are considered to have a rhythmic movement that's linked to the rhythm of the cerebrospinal fluid.

Besides the central nervous system, whose primary components we've listed, the peripheral nervous system is also interconnected with the craniosacral system. It comprises the nerves that extend from the spine to all the ends of the body, whose purpose is to transmit sensory and motor signals.

There's also the autonomic nervous system, which is responsible for the involuntary bodily function that keeps us alive. It's why your heart beats, and your digestion works without your conscious participation. This too, is influenced by the rhythm and health of the craniosacral system.

Last but not least is the endocrine system. The effects of the craniosacral system on the endocrine system are very direct. This is particularly so in the hypothalamus and the pituitary gland, which are vital for hormonal regulation. This means your craniosacral system controls your hormone levels as well, determining your emotional state, sexual function, and so much more.

As you can see, imbalances in the craniosacral system can affect almost every aspect of your well-being, because this system comprises many important organs and tissues, and links to every other organ and bodily function.

Cerebrospinal Fluid and Dura Mater

The cerebrospinal fluid (CSF) and the dura mater, as we've mentioned, are integral parts of the craniosacral system, and the role they play is worth discussing a little further.

CSF primarily protects the brain and spinal cord by cushioning them. It acts as a shock absorber so that in the event of physical trauma, there's a reduced risk of injury to these vital organs. The brain itself is considerably weighty, and it must be kept buoyant so that it floats in the cranial cavity instead of being affected by gravity.

The brain is a living, highly functioning organ, meaning that it needs a source of energy and a way to remove waste. The CSF brings in nutrients such as glucose and electrolytes which the brain uses up in a metabolic process. Once this is done, the waste produced in the brain cells is carried away, again, by the CSF.

The brain and spinal cord need to be in a stable chemical environment, also known as 'homeostasis.' The CSF helps maintain homeostasis by regulating the pH levels and the concentration of various ions within the central nervous system.

The CSF circulates in a pulsating wave around the brain, and that's part of what constitutes the craniosacral rhythm, which, as we've mentioned, can be detected by experienced craniosacral therapists, and used for diagnostic and healing purposes for many issues.

We've mentioned that the dura mater is a protective barrier that contains the cerebrospinal fluid. In addition, it's an attachment point for the veins that drain blood from the brain, so it's vital in regulating intracranial pressure. It's also a supportive framework that helps distribute the mechanical forces in and around the brain, which helps maintain its shape at any given time.

It's the dynamics of the cerebrospinal fluid and the movement of the dura mater that has the most physical influence on the craniosacral rhythm.

Self-Regulation of the Craniosacral System

Central to the philosophy of craniosacral therapy is the idea that the craniosacral system has the ability to regulate itself. These self-regulating capabilities are worth understanding before you learn the techniques of the therapy.

There are various innate self-healing mechanisms that are housed in the craniosacral system. They maintain the health and function of the system and can heal other parts of the body as well. The craniosacral rhythm itself can be understood as the manifestation of the self-regulating abilities of this system. It's the expression of the body's inherent vitality and capacity to heal itself.

The rhythmic flow of the cerebrospinal fluid, the homeostasis it creates, and other automatic functions all occur as part of self-healing and self-regulation.

This self-healing property extends to the rest of the body, through the nervous system, and even further as it is capable of inducing emotional release and healing even psychological issues.

This highlights what's special about craniosacral therapy compared to other forms of holistic healing. Here, it's the body itself that does the healing. The therapist merely unblocks impediments to this natural system by using a gentle touch to release tension and restriction in the craniosacral system.

Biodynamic Craniosacral Therapy

In holistic practices, 'biodynamic' refers to the interconnection between the mind, body, and spirit, and how it can be used to heal and enhance wellbeing. The term biodynamic comes from "bios" which means life, and "dynamics" which refers to the energetic and change-prone nature of the processes that are characteristic of life.

The psychologists and psychotherapists of the 20th century are the ones who pioneered the general concept of biodynamic therapy. Unlike conventional medical practitioners of their time, they emphasized the importance of sensations, emotions, and the psychological state of one's well-being.

For instance, Wilhelm Reich coined the concept of "character armor," the notion that one's emotional and psychological conflicts could be trapped and stored within their body, and that would manifest itself as physical and emotional stress[v].

Later on, a student of Wilhelm named Alexander Lowen developed "bioenergetics," a form of psychotherapy that was oriented around the body, with a focus on releasing physical and emotional tension through specific physical techniques and movements[vi].

Biodynamic Psychology was developed by Gerda Boyesen, a Norwegian physiotherapist, who emphasized the healing power of the rhythmic and pulsating movements of the body as a means of releasing emotional and physical tension[vii].

Biodynamic Rhythm

In the philosophy of craniosacral therapy, the body is considered to have a biodynamic rhythm. This is known as the 'breath of life' because it's the primary respiratory mechanism that keeps us alive. It's understood as the foundational expression of life itself. This rhythm has an inherent healing property and it establishes health and balance.

The biodynamic rhythm, when sensed or 'listened to,' can be a diagnostic tool (meaning it can tell us what's wrong), and it can be the therapeutic target (meaning it could have irregularities that may need restoration to facilitate healing).

The whole objective of craniosacral therapy is to address the restrictions and disruptions in the biodynamic rhythm. Self-healing is put into effect when the touch is used to return this rhythm to its natural balanced state.

The 'breath of life' is understood in slightly differing ways in different holistic practices. In craniosacral therapy, it's seen as a vital force that animates the body, giving it life, vitality, and energy. In this regard, it's similar to the Eastern concept of lifeforce known as Chi (Qi).

The breath of life is a reservoir of healing potential that resides within the body. Anyone can connect to it, but craniosacral therapists have an easier time doing that because they have spent time cultivating energetic awareness. This means they have a heightened sense of the energy fields around themselves and others.

The Principles of Biodynamic Therapy

The following are the key concepts you need to understand in order to grasp biodynamic therapy:

The integration of the body and mind - The core idea, as mentioned, is that the body and mind are intrinsically connected. The physical body contains in it, the key to understanding and resolving psychological and emotional issues.

Release, and transformation - The objective is to release tension, trauma, and emotional blockages all of which are held in the body. This release leads to emotional healing and transformation.

Being attuned to the body - to practice biodynamic therapy, whether on your own or with a therapist, you must be attuned to your bodily sensations, including, your emotions, what your senses take in, and the subtle energy fields within and around you.

Mindful presence - Biodynamic therapy requires mindfulness. This means you have to be present at the moment and fully accept your experiences without judgment. Lack of mindful presence is a blockage to most forms of holistic healing.

The balancing of life energy - The concept of biodynamic therapy works similarly to the Eastern understanding of life energy. The goal is to balance and harmonize this energy, to enhance vitality and wellbeing.

Finally, the principle of a gentle and non-invasive approach applies here as well. Biodynamic therapy uses touch, movement, and breath work to facilitate emotional release and healing.

Biodynamic therapy is "somatic," meaning it's "of the body." There are many therapies like it that address psychological and emotional issues, not by talking, but through rebalancing the body. Somatic therapies are widely integrated into mental health practices and settings, and they've been known to help people through emotional healing and personal growth.

The Breath of Life

The term "breath of life" comes up a lot in several holistic healing modalities, but especially so in craniosacral and biodynamic therapy. It's a fundamental concept that encompasses several key things.

To begin with, it refers to the vital life force, or rather the "subtle life force," that life energy that animates living beings. It's a source of energy, life, and vitality that supports our existence in the physical, emotional, and spiritual dimensions.

Secondly, the breath of life carries a reservoir of healing energy, and it's the same thing as the craniosacral rhythm. It is, however, described in more spiritual terms, as a vessel or medium for a deeper life force, one that connects individuals to a greater sense of purpose and cosmic wisdom.

For these reasons, some craniosacral therapy practitioners refer to what they do as "the breath of life therapy."

The body has an inherent "wisdom" and its ability to heal itself is just a part of that. You can "tune" into this body wisdom by carrying out body-of-life exercises, which mostly consist of deeply meditative and self-awareness exercises.

Breath of Life Exercises

Most craniosacral exercises have similar preparatory steps. The first is to take a comfortable and relaxing position in a peaceful place (usually lying or sitting down in a designated place at a therapist's office). The second is to establish a sense of grounding and relaxation, usually through breathing and centering exercises, to facilitate a calm and focused mind.

After you are in a well prepared state, here are some exercises to tune into the breath of life. These are simple enough that you can do them on your own.

Mindful breathing -
- Find a serene place and sit or lie down comfortably.
- Close your eyes, and take a few deep breaths to center yourself.
- Pay close attention to your breathing.
- When you breathe in and out, notice any subtle sensations in your body.
- Focus on the rise and fall of your chest and the expansion and contraction of your abdomen.
- Try to connect with the rhythm of your breath, and the idea that it gives you life.

The body-scan meditation -
- Lie down comfortably, with eyes closed, and take deep breaths.
- Focus your mind on your toes as you breathe.
- After lingering on your toes for a while, shift your focus upwards slowly, as you progressively scan your body and narrowly focus on any sensations you find along the way.
- Pay particular attention to areas of tension.
- As you move through each part of the body, imagine you are breathing life force into that part,

and this breath of life is blowing away and releasing tension and stress.

- Pay extra attention to the cranial area, the spine, and the sacrum, as you explore the subtle rhythm of the craniosacral system.

Basic visualization exercise -

- In a quiet, peaceful place, sit down with your eyes closed and visualize a gentle, rhythmic way of energy passing through your body.
- Picture it as the breath of life.
- Envision it emanating from the core of your being and flowing outward towards the edges of the body.
- Picture it cleansing, healing, and nourishing every organ in your body to the cellular level.

Self-massage using the gentle touch -

- Sit down in the lotus position, or comfortably in a chair with a relaxed posture.
- Lightly tap or stroke various parts of your body, starting with your face and head, then slowly moving down to your neck, chest, and abdomen.
- As you do this, visualize the touch stimulating the breath of life within you, awakening the inner energy and vitality.
- Ensure you are present and mindful to fully experience the sensations.

Harmonizing the Energetic Body

There's a very ancient belief that originates in the East, that the human body has a subtle energy system, which determines our physical, emotional, and spiritual well-being.

This energy system comprises interconnected energy centers called chakras. Each of these energy centers is responsible for certain parts of the body, and the wellness outcomes that correspond to those parts.

Chakras are visualized as five spinning wheels of energy, spaced out at different points along the spine, with the sixth located at the forehead, and the seventh at the crown (top) of the head.

In addition to the energy centers, there are subtle bodies (known as auras) that are within the body or those that engulf it, and they too have an impact on our state of being.

Auras are described as electromagnetic fields of energy that extend beyond the physical body itself and reflect our emotions, thoughts, and wellness. Auras come in layers, each with a spiritual and corporal purpose.

There's also Kundalini energy which, in Hindu tradition, is believed to reside at the base of the spine (the sacrum) and shoot upwards when activated, revitalizing the body.

Prana, a similar kind of energy, is considered the life force energy in Indian tradition. Prana has similarities with Chi (Qi), the life force energy in Chinese spirituality and medicine. Both Prana and Qi are central to maintaining the health and balance of living things.

In holistic practices such as acupuncture and acupressure, it's believed that energy meridians traverse the body, and are pathways through which life energy (Prana or Qi) flows.

While the frameworks of understanding were developed independently across space and time, these forms of energy are comparable to the breath of life and craniosacral rhythm that we are focusing on in this book. In craniosacral therapy, part of the objective is to harmonize the energetic body, no matter what framework of understanding you follow.

Chakras, energy meridians, or other energy centers, have long been believed to be connected to the central nervous system, which means they literally intersect with the craniosacral system which includes the spine, brain, and cerebrospinal fluid and membranes that engulf it.

Harmonizing the energetic body involves releasing blockages, through gentle touch and manipulation techniques which block the flow of energy, leading to emotional imbalances and physical issues. Many craniosacral therapists have a functional understanding of chakras, and they use touch techniques to rebalance and align them.

If the energetic body is in a state of disharmony, the self-healing capacity of the craniosacral system is impaired. You may experience a disordered life force, a lack of homeostasis to support proper central nervous system function, and problems with your immunity. You may also experience negative and distressing emotions.

Energetic healing is an ancient practice that has seen a resurgence as people in the West have warmed up to Eastern spiritual ideas. Besides touch therapy (a core aspect of craniosacral therapy), practices like Reiki also work with subtle energy fields to promote healing. Trained practitioners use their hands to strategically influence the flow of energy in the body, fixing the ailment or issue in question.

Energy Balancing

Energy balancing is common in craniosacral therapy. Its aim is to restore harmony and promote the flow of energy within the subtle energy systems in the body. Here's a step-by-step explanation of how energy balancing is typically done in a session of craniosacral therapy:

You will lie on your back on a sturdy adjustment table in your therapist's office. You won't have to change your clothes or undress as this is all non-invasive. You just need to be relaxed, comfortable, and well-supported.

Your therapist will give you prompts on how to ground yourself, and be present in the moment for the procedure to work as intended. Energy balancing requires a calm state of mind.

The therapist will assess your energy fields by placing their hands very lightly on your body. They'll focus mostly on your energy centers (chakras), or the energy meridians.

Using a light touch, your therapist will scan these energy centers and fields to sense any disturbances, blocks, or imbalances. Some holistic healers will use their training, while others may have natural spiritual abilities to detect problems with energy fields.

Holistic healers who work with chakras can tell if your energy isn't flowing correctly if it's emitting the right or wrong color, if it's vibrant enough or is diminished, if the energy is overactive or underactive, and so on.

These attributes tell the healer what imbalances are at play, and what needs to be done. Experienced healers will also know if the energy imbalance is related to an emotional or a physical problem.

To balance and harmonize the energy, your craniosacral therapist will use the hands-on method, but he/she may also guide you through visualization exercises or intention setting.

Rebalancing energy may involve unblocking energy pathways and sending more energy in the direction of chakras that are depleted. It may also involve releasing the extra energy from a chakra that's overactive.

The therapist will gently manipulate the location of the energy chakra along the spine, and this gentle touch will harmonize the cerebrospinal fluid rhythm in the area and release any block. Manipulation can be done with the goal of encouraging circulation, directing the energy toward a specific target, clearing blocks, or focusing that energy.

Craniosacral therapy touch may be used alongside focused intention, meaning thoughts, visualization, and affirmations to direct the energy and facilitate balancing.

The therapist must keep listening to your body, and also communicate with you verbally to stay on top of shifts in energy patterns and gauge the way you react to the energy balancing work.

It may take several sessions and integration with several other holistic healing techniques for your energy to be wholly rebalanced. But when it's all done, you will be physically, emotionally, and spiritually in harmony.

Craniosacral Therapy Techniques

Craniosacral therapy uses a wide variety of practical techniques to harmonize the energy in the body, with the goal of releasing tension, improving the flow of cerebrospinal fluid, and supporting the self-healing mechanism of the body. Key techniques include:

The Light Touch

The light touch is a foundational technique in craniosacral therapy and it's used to interact with the body's subtle rhythms, assess them, and detect energy patterns. Here's the standard step-by-step process that practitioners follow when using the light touch technique:

Setting the environment

The environment must be quiet and calm to ensure you are relaxed and comfortable. You'll remain, fully clothed, lying on a comfortable treatment table, while the therapist sits on a raised stool, or stands nearby.

Establishing mindfulness

The therapist will center him/herself, and enter into a state of mindful presence, which is required to successfully preside over any craniosacral therapy session.

Hand placement

The practitioner will place their hands gently on a specific area of your body. This usually starts at the head, because it's where the craniosacral rhythm is the most palpable. It's common to place the hands on the cranium, the sacrum, and several other key locations - this is at the discretion of the therapist, and based on the information you provide about the nature of your problem.

The light contact

When the therapist makes contact with your body, it's with the use of a very light touch. The pressure applied through this touch should be no more than 5 grams, or roughly the weight of a nickel. Excess pressure would interfere with the craniosacral rhythm and make it harder to detect.

Sensory awareness

The therapist uses this light touch, either with the tips of the fingers or the entire palm, to "tune" into your body, and feel all the subtle movements, rhythms, and pulsations. Trained therapists can narrow in on the craniosacral rhythm and distinguish it from other sensations emanating from your body.

Making assessments

After tuning in and detecting the craniosacral rhythm, the therapist will maintain the light touch for a while and make assessments about its qualities. For instance, is the craniosacral rhythm symmetrical? Are there areas where it's restricted? Is there an imbalance in the craniosacral system? All areas of imperfection will be identified and noted by the practitioner.

Palpation and release

After the therapist finds and makes note of the restrictions and imbalances, he/she will use a gentle "palpation" technique to nudge the affected area to "release." Palpation is a medical and clinical term that refers to the use of one's hands and fingers to make an examination, usually by applying gentle pressure and touch to find abnormalities and unusual sensations. In craniosacral therapy, palpation does just find problems, it's used to unblock them. Releasing blocks may involve applying gentle compression or making subtle adjustments to the cranial bone, or other components of the craniosacral system.

Listening and responding

The craniosacral therapy process is usually a back-and-forth process where the therapist detects a problem, applies a technique, detects how the craniosacral system responds to the technique, and then doubles down on that technique or switches to one that's more called for. It's not a rigid procedure, it's a responsorial one.

Facilitating self-healing

Recall that craniosacral therapy is founded on the principle that the body has an innate self-healing mechanism, and the whole purpose of the therapy is to support that self-healing process by removing barriers. The light touch and mindful presence are used to nurture the craniosacral system in your body, and after the session, you feel less tense and stressed, and more balanced, both emotionally and physically.

At the end of the session, the therapist will gradually reduce the pressure of the touch, and you will slowly open your eyes and unwind, before getting back to your day.

Listening to the Craniosacral Rhythm

The setting of the environment, preposition, the establishment of a mindful state, and the placement of hands are done in the same way as in the previous technique.

After these stages, the therapist places their hands where the craniosacral rhythm is most readily palpable, and establishes the same light touch as described before.

<u>Attunement to the rhythm</u>

The therapist tunes to the rhythm by paying keen attention to the sensation beneath their hands. The craniosacral rhythm is a subtle and cyclical movement created when the cerebrospinal fluid circulates around the brain and spinal cord. It's distinguishable from other rhythms in the body because it occurs at a rate of about six to twelve cycles every minute. It cannot be confused with the pulse or your breathing. The therapist must attentively feel for the rhythm of your cranium or sacral until he/she gets a beat on it. This may take a while, and how fast it goes depends on the skill and experience of the craniosacral therapist.

<u>Listening to the rhythm</u>

The rhythm, once detected, can be listened to, much as one would listen to vibrations or any other sensations, and from that process, the therapist can discern several things. We've mentioned that the quality and symmetry of the craniosacral rhythm can be assessed and improved. There's also the amplitude of the rhythm, whether the rhythm flows smoothly and freely, and so many more things.

Listening to the rhythm is also done throughout any craniosacral therapy session to monitor for changes and determine improvements, or effectiveness of the techniques being used.

Usually, after listening to the craniosacral rhythm, the therapist may tell you certain things about your health and emotional well-being and may ask you to make certain changes or take up specific holistic practices in your life.

Cranial Bone Manipulation

We've mentioned that much of craniosacral therapy is about cranial bone manipulation, i.e. the practice of applying small amounts of pressure on the bones that make up the cranium to restore the self-healing ability of the craniosacral system. Here is how that manipulation is done.

The initial preparatory steps are similar, except in this technique, extra care is taken to ensure that you are not just relaxed and comfortable, but well supported as you lie on your back. The craniosacral therapist has to be present and mindful, but also highly focused.

Hand placement

The therapist will place their hands on your head, particularly, on the cranial bones. Therapists are trained to understand the bones that make up the cranium, i.e., the frontal, temporal, parietal, and occipital bones.

Making an assessment

The therapist will use the light touch, this time to assess the cranial bones and the structure around them for signs of restriction, misalignment, or tension in general. Using palpation, the therapist will find any subtle movements or asymmetries that are out of the ordinary, and judge whether cranial bones need to be manipulated to resolve it.

The therapist will pay particular attention to any areas of the cranial bone that feel restricted or tense. Such areas will not be moving in harmony with the natural craniosacral rhythm. You may even feel slight discomfort when the practitioner touches these areas, and you should verbally describe any such discomfort to the practitioner to help with the assessment.

<u>The gentle manipulation of cranial bones</u>

If the therapist determines that it's necessary, he/she will use very gentle and precise manipulation techniques to ever so slightly move the cranial bones and release the tension. Typically, the touch is very subtle and non-invasive. Extra special care must be taken if the procedure is done on small children (who have soft skulls) or people who have experienced head trauma in the past, have undergone brain surgery, or suffer chronic headaches.

The therapist also makes a determination of the direction of movement that needs to occur for the tension to be relieved. This is done following the craniosacral rhythm and the body's own wisdom. Once the direction is determined, the therapist will use gentle pressure, subtle movement, and traction to move the bones, so mildly, that most patients don't typically feel it happen.

The therapist must keep listening and sensing throughout the process to feel any changes to the cranial bone and figure out if the release has occurred. This constant monitoring is also a safety measure as it prevents the effects of any previous misjudgment from compounding.

In a cranial bone manipulation session, the therapist will talk to you constantly and ask how you feel throughout. This is to ensure you remain comfortable, and you help inform the therapist's approach to ensure the best outcome.

Manipulating the bones of the skull may sound like an invasive thing, but it really isn't. Experienced craniosacral therapists will perform this procedure with sensitivity and precision, and it's no risk at all.

Fascial Unwinding

First, what is fascia, and why does it need unwinding?

Fascia is a thin casing of connective tissue that forms a web that spreads all across the body. It's responsible for holding everything in the body, including organs, bones, nerve fiber, muscle fiber, and blood vessels in place, and therefore providing the body with much of its internal structure. It's because of fascia that your body organs don't collapse in on each other, but are able to maintain their shape and integrity.

Fascia also protects the body's internal organs and microstructures from external shock. It also contributes to the function of the muscles, by enabling them to transmit force, and to work in coordination with each other, giving you motor function.

Fascia also encases nerves, protecting them and ensuring their proper function of sending signals all across the body. Fascia is important for the distribution of fluids within the body as well.

However, the fascia has nerves running through it, which makes it very sensitive. It's believed to be as sensitive as skin, if not more so. So, when you are stressed, the fascia throughout your body senses the stress, and it tightens.

Stress triggers your fight, flight, or freeze response, and the hormone cortisol is released. The stress hormone causes tension in muscles and higher nerve activity, and the fascia contracts and tightens in an attempt to protect the body. As a result, you feel stiff, discomfort, even pain.

The problem gets worse if the stress is prolonged to the point of being chronic. It could be manifested as musculoskeletal issues, like tension headaches and back pain.

Craniosacral therapy is one of several release techniques for tightened fascia.

The unwinding process

The therapy session starts with the preparation process where you lie in a supported manner on your back, while the therapist centers him/herself.

The therapist uses gentle touch to assess the fascia and find areas of tension. He/she will then initiate movement of the fascia. This involves gently massaging and stretching the fascia in the direction it needs to go to unwind itself.

The body itself gives natural cues, through the craniosacral rhythm, and the nature and the extent of the fascial tension. It's also the body that determines the pace and direction with which the unwinding occurs.

The fascial unwinding process is fluid and rhythmic, and the therapist will synchronize to this rhythm as she gently guides the fascia towards unknotting and healing itself.

As the session goes on, you will feel less tense in the areas that the therapist has worked on, as she progressively goes over from one point of tension to another.

After the fascial unwinding or the myofascial release therapy session, you should feel improved mobility as your body recovers its natural healing abilities. The emotional distress that caused the tension may also reside.

Sacral Rocking

Sacral rocking is a technique used in various forms of physical therapy, including chiropractic care and craniosacral therapy. It involves moving the sacrum in a gentle and rhythmic fashion to adjust it. The sacrum is an important part of the pelvis and the spinal cord, and it supports much of the weight of the upper body, it is crucial in transmitting that weight to the limbs.

Sacral rocking is used to address issues such as lower back pain, dysfunction in the pelvic area (such as misalignment that causes pain in the hips), pelvic joint problems (which lead to mobility issues), and circulation problems in the tissue around the area.

The aim of sacral rocking is to relieve tension, realign the sacrum, restore mobility, and facilitate relaxation. Mobility in the pelvic area has a bearing on sexual function, so sacral rocking can help improve the sex lives of clients.

The sacrum is a small triangular bone at the base of the spine, and that's why the therapist puts her focus. The preparation steps are similar to those we've already encountered. You lie on the treatment table in a comfortable and well-supported position, and the therapist prepares by centering herself.

The therapist gently places her hand on your body around the sacrum and lower back area. She'll use palpation to evaluate the sacral area and detect any tension or restrictions there. This is done by listening to the craniosacral rhythm, observing your reaction to the touch, or asking you to explain how you feel when the palpation is carried out. She'll then make note of all the areas of tightness.

The therapist may also ask you questions about your mobility, or the nature of your back pain if that's what brought you to their office.

The sacral rocking technique

The therapist will place both hands gently over the sacrum, and create a slow, gentle rhythmic rocking movement on the bone. The movement is either horizontal, vertical, or cyclical, depending on how the therapist has assessed your needs. As she does this, the therapist will also pay keen attention to your natural rhythm and the cues from your body. She will encourage you to try and relax so that you don't stiffen or move involuntarily, interfering with the treatment. If all goes as intended, circulation will improve in the sacral area and you will feel a sense of ease as tension is released.

Breathwork

Most holistic practices incorporate a lot of breathwork, and craniosacral therapy is no exception. It contributes to relaxation, which is necessary to enhance the therapeutic process, and release tension. Let's look at some of the most common breathwork techniques used in craniosacral therapy sessions.

Diaphragmatic breathing

This refers to deep abdominal breaths whose purpose is to reduce stress and tension and foster relaxation. It involves the following steps:

- Lie down on your back and in a comfortable position.
- Take slow, deep breaths by expanding your thorax as far as it can go with each inhalation, then slowly letting it contract with each exhalation.

The benefit of diaphragmatic breathing is that it activates the parasympathetic nervous system, which is why it induces a state of relaxation.

Somatic experiencing breathwork

The purpose of somatic experiencing breathwork is to release stored physical and emotional tension, which allows you to fully experience or express bodily sensation. Sensation is important in craniosacral therapy and all forms of holistic healing because you must be attuned to your body to know if the healing is working. The following steps are involved in this breathwork technique:

- Take slow and deep breaths, while paying close attention to all the sensations in your body, especially those in the craniosacral system.
- Take slow and deep breaths, this time paying close attention to the emotions that arise.
- Focus on a specific area of tension, or a specific negative emotion, and feel it releasing or dissipating with each exhalation.
- Focus on the natural movements and sounds that occur as you breathe. This will ground and relax you further.

Somatic experiencing breathwork helps you process and release a lot of tension and trauma that's been accumulated and stored in your body. It provides relief of both a physical and emotional nature.

Balanced breathing

The aim of the balanced breath technique is to create a harmonious rhythm of inhalation and exhalation, for a considerable period of time. This way, it balances the autonomic nervous system and improves your well-being. The steps involved in the balanced breath technique are as follows:

- Test your lung capacity to establish how long you are able to breathe in and out. This is especially important to establish for people with respiratory issues and diseases.

- Inhale for the specific count that you've chosen, then exhale for the same count.
- Repeat this breathing pattern at a consistent pace. In a craniosacral therapy session, your breathing may be guided in such a way that it's synchronized to a gentle movement or an imagery of the therapist's choosing. At home, you can synchronize your breath to the ticking of a clock or a metronome app on your phone.
- Be mindful and present as you do this breathwork, and you can do it for as long as you want.

The balanced breath will help your body find a state of equilibrium. It will cut down on stress, and increase your mental clarity.

Four-part breath

The four-part breath technique is designed to give emphasis to four distinct phases of your breathing cycle. It's meant to help you commence with different aspects of the breathing experience, making you more mindful, present, and in control. The steps involved are as follows:

- Breathe in deeply, making sure to maximally fill your lower abdomen with air first, your mid-abdomen second, your upper chest third, and then your collarbones last.
- Breathe out, releasing the air in the reverse order, this time, your collarbones first, your chest second, your mid-abdomen third, and your lower abdomen last.

This improves your breathing control and trains you to properly carry out most other breathwork exercises.

Ujjayi breath technique

This is a yogic form of breathing where you create soft oceanic sounds as you breathe, with the aim of increasing both concentration and relaxation. The steps involved are as follows:

- Breathe through the nose as you slightly constrict the back of your throat. This should generate a gentle ocean wave sound.
- Make sure your breathing is slow, smooth, deep, and very controlled.
- Keep breathing in this rhythmic pattern for as long as you are okay doing it.

Yogis swear by Ujjayi breath, and they believe it calms the mind and treats anxiety. You can do it even when sitting at your desk at work. It can be enhanced by closing your eyes and picturing yourself sitting on a serene beach.

Visualization

We've mentioned that visualization techniques are sometimes used in craniosacral therapy, so let's look at that in some detail. The incorporation of visualization is rooted in the holistic principle that the mind, body, and spirit are all connected. Mental imagery (something that exists just in the mind) can promote balance and relaxation in the physical body, and create harmony between the corporal body and the energy fields that traverse it.

As with everything else, a visualization session starts with preparation. You lie comfortably in a relaxed and supported manner on the treatment table.

The therapist will prepare herself, through grounding techniques, and then she'll set the intention for the session. The intention set will depend on your specific needs according to interviews you've had with the therapist or the diagnosis she's made from examining your craniosacral system or assessing your energy state.

The therapist will place her hands on the area of concern during some visualization exercises, while other exercises may not require contact at all.

Guided visualization involves the use of calming and descriptive language to lead one into a state of deep relaxation. There's usually a theme that goes with each visualization exercise, and this may depend on your preference or the preferences of the therapist. Common themes include; a peaceful natural setting, a vision of blockages or tension being released, a vision of a healing light permeating the body, and so much more.

You will be encouraged to engage all of your senses during the visualization exercises. For example, if you are visualizing a natural setting, you need to picture what it looks like, hear how it sounds, sense how it smells, feel the air on your skin, and hear the sounds from the surroundings. Good visualization is multisensory, and immersive, it just requires the ability to focus your mind on the visual.

The therapist will also inquire, not just about the sensations, but how the vision makes you feel emotionally, experientially, and so on.

In craniosacral therapy, the therapist may find a point of tension in your body and ask you to visualize the body's innate healing property, in the form of a cleansing fluid or a brilliant light, washing over that point, and restoring energy flow through it. The therapist may simultaneously carry out palpation or other adjustments as you do your visualization. Tapping into this mind-body connection enhances the effectiveness of craniosacral therapy.

At the closure of the visualization exercise, the therapist will slowly guide you to bring your awareness back to your physical environment.

The success of a visualization session depends on two things. First, the skill of the therapist, and second, your receptivity toward the process. That's why it requires an open mind on your part to fully benefit from this kind of therapy. Skeptics who disregard the guidance of the therapist rarely see positive outcomes in this process.

Resolving Trauma

If you've lived through a major traumatic event in your life, you are not alone. Roughly 70% of adults across the world have experienced major trauma at least once in their lives. But most trauma goes untreated and therefore unresolved, and that weighs heavily on the physical and mental health of many individuals. Craniosacral therapy might be the key to resolving your trauma.

How? We've already talked about the body's self-healing property that lies in the craniosacral system, and that the physical body stores trauma within itself. The capacity of your flesh to store trauma is known as tissue intelligence, and these memories of trauma are manifested as imbalances in the craniosacral system and physical discomfort in the body.

You've heard it said that the body remembers. The stored trauma causes constant or dormant dysfunction or discomfort. Dormant traumatic memories can be triggered by new events, and old pain can resurface.

The craniosacral system contains the imprint of every bit of trauma you've encountered in your life, and if there's been a lot of trauma, then the functioning of the system is affected. If you feel disconnected from your own bodily sensations, or you always feel unsafe and unable to relax, then you might harbor a lot of trauma in your tissue.

This imprinted trauma, as we discussed, causes complex health issues, which worsen with chronic exposure. You may have muscular tension, problems with your autonomic nervous system, inflammation-related ailments, a damaged immune system, and dysfunctional organs.

And yet, every time you have a fight or flight reaction to frightening events, you experience stress and tension at work, or you go through any neurological changes, the trauma adds up, piling in your tissue.

Unresolved, this could lead to chronic physical pain, mental health issues, heart disease, and other cardiovascular issues, suppression of your immune response to infections, and the impairment of your interpersonal relationship, which could damage your social life.

Craniosacral therapy has an answer for all this.

All the craniosacral techniques we've discussed so far can contribute toward resolving trauma. If you go in for a session, your therapist will use the light touch to listen to your system's subtle rhythms and locate the damage that the trauma has done to your body. She'll then do what's known as somatic tracking, which involves following the sensations in your body to find the holding patterns of the trauma.

The therapist may also carry out still point induction, where she induces your craniosacral rhythm into a moment of stillness, so that it takes a pause, allowing your body to reset itself. When the rhythm restarts, your stored tension will be released and the system goes back to functioning normally.

The therapist may also resolve your trauma by applying techniques to enhance fluid dynamics in your cerebrospinal fluid, encouraging flow and movement, with the goal of creating relaxation. She may also unblock stagnant energy associated with the exact cause or outcome of your trauma. She may carry out treatments that involve spontaneous and therapeutic movements of your body in order to unwind it.

There are many trauma-release exercises that originate from the practice of craniosacral therapy, as well as holistic healing. There are even others that are used in mainstream physiotherapy for the same purpose. A lot of these exercises are highly technical and require a professional's help to perform. However, there are some that you can carry out on your own.

Here are three trauma-resolving exercises that you can do at home.

Somatic Awareness Exercise

This exercise is meant to increase awareness of your own body. A mindful self-awareness tunes you into your bodily sensations and anchors you in the present moment. This way, you can make non-judgmental observations about yourself, and create a compassionate space where you acknowledge and accept the current state of your body. In connecting with the self, your mind and body merge and you can understand your areas of tension and trauma.

The steps are as follows:
- Find a quiet and comfortable place, and sit or lie down.
- Close your eyes and breathe as deeply as you comfortably can to center yourself.
- Recall any areas in your body where you experienced physical injury, and focus on those parts, one after another.
- Notice any sensations on that part of the body, whether it is mild discomfort or deep pain.

47

- Take time and scan the whole body to find all areas of both physical and emotional trauma, and focus your mind on, acknowledging what you are finding and recalling the related experience, then letting it go.

Gentle Neck Release Exercise

The purpose of this exercise is to release the tension around the neck. The muscles of the neck and shoulders hold more tension and stress than most other parts of the body, and they need special focus. The neck supports the cranium (skull), and if it's stiff, it interferes with the wellness of the craniosacral system. This exercise enables you to increase the range of motion of your neck and promote flexibility. You should accompany it with deep breathing as you stretch your neck to stimulate further relaxation and a sense of calm.

To perform gentle neck release exercises, follow these steps:
- Sit comfortably on a chair or on the floor (lotus position).
- Slowly and progressively tilt your head on one side, as though you are bringing your ear down to touch your shoulder.
- Put your hand on the opposite side of the head, and gently but steadily apply pressure to enhance your stretch.
- Take deep breaths, and hold your head in this position for roughly 30 seconds.
- Reduce the pressure you are applying on your head, and slowly return to the neutral position.
- Repeat this exercise doing every step this time in the opposite direction.

Stillness and Self-Folding Exercise

The purpose of this exercise is to soothe yourself by placing your hands, your heart, and your abdominal area in a self-folding gesture. This makes you feel a sense of self-love, comfort, and safety. You have to connect this gesture with your breathing, to anchor your attention to the present moment.

Follow these steps:

Lie down comfortably on your back.

Place your right hand across your chest and over your heart, and the left hand over your abdomen. You can switch up the hands if you are more comfortable that way, but one hand must cross the heart.

Close your eyes and relax, focus on your breathing. Don't try to control your breath, let it settle at a slow natural pace that's typical of a person in a state of rest.

Let your body become still, and let go of any unnecessary tension.

Pay attention to any sensations or subtle movements, but just make a mental note of them, don't try to change them.

Boosting Tissue Intelligence

Your body's innate capacity to self-regulate and heal itself is something you should aim to boost. But how can you go about doing that?

The mindfulness, awareness, breathwork, and relaxation exercises we've discussed so far can go a long way in helping increase your tissue intelligence. However good wellness practices also contribute to higher tissue intelligence. For instance, people who exercise and move more frequently are better off than those who do. It's why practices such as yoga and tai chi are leading boosters of tissue intelligence.

Good nutrition and adequate hydration are also important. Remember that the cerebrospinal fluid functions best when it has the required nutrients to nourish the brain and spine, and when your body has enough hydration for its internal fluid dynamics to work optimally.

Self-care and good quality sleep also boost tissue intelligence and provide the body with the conditions necessary to heal itself.

You should work on expressing your emotions instead of bottling them up because accumulated negative emotion creates blockages that cause dysfunction in the craniosacral system. Activities such as journaling, and connecting with nature have also been known to boost tissue intelligence.

Conclusion

Thanks for reading *Craniosacral Therapy 101*. You are now familiar with all the introductory concepts of craniosacral therapy, and can even perform some of the basic exercises that are related to this holistic therapy practice.

To fully benefit from this therapy, you need to see a licensed professional who can help with whatever physiological or emotional issue you need resolved. For now, use the exercises contained in this book to help boost your craniosacral health, and cope with everyday stresses and past trauma.

Practice makes perfect, so the more you try out these exercises, the better you'll get at them, and the more your holistic benefits will accrue.

Remember that within your body lies the power of self-healing, and it's in keeping an open mind and learning more about holistic approaches, that you unlock that power.

Thanks again, and Namaste.

References

[i] Wales, Anne L. (1990). *Teachings in the science of osteopathy.* Cambridge, MA: Rudra Press.

[ii] Upledger, John E (1995). *"Craniosacral Therapy".* Physical Therapy. 75 (4): 328–30. doi:10.1093/ptj/75.4.328. PMID 7899490

[iii] Evidence-based health *care and complementary and alternative medicine. (2016). Evidence-Based Healthcare in Context,* 131–150. https://doi.org/10.4324/9781315255774-17

[iv] Haller H, Lauche R, Sundberg T, Dobos G, Cramer H (December 2019). "Craniosacral therapy for chronic pain: a systematic review and meta-analysis of randomized controlled trials". BMC Musculoskelet Disord. 21 (1): 1. doi:10.1186/s12891-019-3017-y

[v] Samsel, M. (n.d.). Finding feeling and purpose by Michael Samsel. Armor. https://www.reichandlowentherapy.org/Content/Energy_and_Mo vement/armor.html

[vi] What is bioenergetics?. Lowen Foundation. (n.d.). https://www.lowenfoundation.org/what-is-bioenergetics

[vii] Dr. Elya Steinberg M.D., Transformative Moments: Short Stories from the Biodynamic Psychotherapy Room.

Printed in Great Britain
by Amazon

54221780R00036